THE MOST PRECIOUS GIFT

Devotional prose and poetry

by

Dolly Sewell

MOORLEY'S Print & Publishing

All good gifts around us
Are sent from heaven above,
Then thank the Lord, O thank the Lord
For all His love.

© Copyright 1996.

ISBN 0 86071 459 4

MOORLEY'S Print & Publishing

23 Park Rd., Ilkeston, Derbys DE7 5DA
Tel/Fax: (0115) 932 0643

DOLLY SEWELL is a prolific writer. Her articles, short stories, features, regular columns, religious features and poetry have been published in books, magazines and newspapers in this country and in various countries overseas, especially the USA. At one time she did quite a lot of broadcasting on the BBC. She is a Contributing Editor on the magazine ABUNDANT LIVING, published in Arizona, America, and a contributor to PRAIRIE TIMES, Colorado, USA.

At one time she wrote pantomimes, one being in mime for the Deaf and Dumb.

To date this is her tenth book, including several books of puzzles. She compiles puzzle books for the League of Friends of University Hospital - Queen's Medical Centre, and does all the selling.

She is passionately fond of travelling and adventure. When she was 66 she piloted a plane in Oregon, USA, and is the proud possessor of a Pilot's Log Book. To celebrate her 75th birthday she did a sponsored balloon flight for the PDSA, and celebrated her 80th birthday with a microlight flight, raising £1,547.59 toward the new Day Centre for Children with Cancer at the University Hospital.

Just prior to her 76th birthday, quite accidentally, she took up painting, and - so far - has had 8 exhibitions of her water colours and is selling well.

Dolly is a Life Member and Vice President of the Nottingham Writers' Club.

CONTENTS

The end of page fillers are original Japanese-style haikus by the author.

THE MOST PRECIOUS GIFT

The appetizing odour of freshly-baked oat-cakes gifted Benjamin's nostrils as he walked into the house, his pet lamb trotting meekly at his heels.

"*They smell good, Mother,*" he said, conscious of the saliva on his tongue. "*May I have one while it is still hot?*"

Phoebe turned from the hot stone slab, beneath which the charcoal fire burned redly. She was tired. The flour had needed pounding until it was fine as silk and the goat milked so that the milk could be used while it was still warm. But she had a smile for her son. Nine-year-old Benjamin had spelled joy for her from the moment of his birth.

She nodded. "*Just one. Do not burn yourself.*"

Soon Benjamin's shining white teeth were sinking into its goodness. "*M-mm! The best ever. How Father would enjoy these.*" Then he had a thought. "*He'll be minding the sheep on the hillside. I'll take some to him.*"

"*No, my son. The journey would take many hours. You might lose your way.*"

"*I have made the journey many times,*" he urged. "*My lamb will keep me company.*"

His mother looked into the pleading brown eyes, and gave in. She wrapped four oat-cakes in a piece of coarse linen, put them in a goatskin bag and, gently pushing him to the door, said: "*God be with you and with your lamb.*"

Benjamin skipped and ran, the lamb frisking at his side, baaing contentedly, "*Baa-baa*" imitated Benjamin. "*Is that all you have to say?*" and he stopped a moment to hug the woolly white head, remembering with joy the day his father had given the lamb to him. "*Here's a friend for you, my son,*" he had said. Their nearest neighbour was a donkey ride away, and Benjamin an only child.

The sun shone hotly from a cloudless blue sky. The boy and his lamb travelled through olive groves and sandy wastes, through fields and across tiny streams. As he jumped, the goatskin bag bounced on his back. At last the sun sank in a turquoise coloured sky. One moment it looked like an enormous blood orange, the next it had gone, leaving behind a colour like squashed grapes. The lamb bleated.

"*Am I going too fast for you?*" Benjamin asked his friend. Laughingly he picked the lamb up in his arms and carried it close, warm against his heart. Already darkness had fallen, but the risen moon, pale as a lemon, showed the way. Then, just as Benjamin's arms were aching almost unbearably, he saw the shepherds.

"*Father!*" he cried. And turning to the lamb added: "*Look how tall my father is. Taller than all the other .....*" The words died in his throat. How light it was becoming! As he watched, a great white light seemed to fill the sky. Holding the lamb close, panic beating drum-like in his breast, he started to run. Light now poured like liquid silver from the heavens. He dropped to his knees, shielding his eyes with a shaking hand, the other tight around the lamb. As he looked again, mesmerized, at the bright light, the centre of it formed into an angel.

"*Fear not,*" came the voice, "*for behold I bring you tidings of great joy. For unto you is born this day in the city of David a Saviour, which is Christ the Lord. And this shall be a sign unto you. You shall find the babe wrapped in swaddling clothes and lying in a manger.*"

Benjamin gasped, and hid his face in the lamb's white coat. When, at last, he dared to lift his head again, the great light had gone. But overhead, was a star of unusual brightness. His father's voice carried to him across the lonely hillside. "*See! The star points the way. Let us go into the city and find the new babe.*"

The words "*Wait for me, Father,*" were already on Benjamin's lips, as he started to run ..... But, supposing his father said that it was too late for his young son to be out? Supposing he was sent back to his mother? What then? For one did not disobey one's father.

"*Sh!*" he bade the lamb and, keeping in the shadows, he followed the shepherds, his eye on the shining star which, miraculously, seemed to be showing the way. Now they were entering the city. The star hung low, seeming to stop above a stable, close by an inn. Oblivious of everything, including the astonished voice of his father calling, "*Son! Son!*" Benjamin ran as fast as he could, handicapped by the weight of the lamb.

The stable door was open. He peeped in. "*It is the Holy Babe and his mother!*" he whispered to the lamb. "*And three men in silken robes, each wearing a crown.*" Even as he spoke, the first king presented a gift of gold, bowed, and withdrew. The second king, head bowed in humility, gave frankincense. The third, tall, black and powerful-looking, magnificent in a scarlet robe, presented myrrh.

Panic ebbed and flowed in Benjamin's heart, like sand in a wind-swept desert. Presents for the new-born babe. How special this baby must be. *"A Saviour,"* the Angel had said. *"Christ the Lord."* Unfamiliar tears stung his eyes. He wanted to go up to that manger. He wanted to bow before the baby. But how could he? Surely a gift for a Saviour should be beyond price. And he had nothing.

He turned away, misery searing his heart. Then he stopped in his tracks. *"A gift beyond price."* Without a word - for they seemed to have stuck in his throat - he moved forward and held out his lamb to the Holy Babe. Then, as gently as a mother with a beloved child, he laid the snowy creature at the foot of the manger.

Immediately he was up and running, running, running ..... Running through the door, past the shepherds, past his father, out into the cool, starlit night. And, as he ran, and in spite of the tears that flowed down his cheeks, a song of joy leapt and swelled in his heart. For had not he given the Baby Saviour the most precious gift of all? His only friend.

Spring came in a blaze of scarlet and gold brilliance and fired me with hope.

ALL GOOD GIFTS AROUND US

In Church and Chapel throughout all the land
An annual Harvest Festival takes place,
When special hymns are sung and prayers said:
A service of Thanksgiving and of Praise.
The fruits of field and orchard are all there:
The wheat and rye, the turnip, grape and plum,
Tomatoes, apples, carrot, cauliflower,
Bright dahlias, sweetpeas ..... and pots of jam.
All are arranged with tender, loving care
Along the altar rail and window sill,
Communion table, steps and organ top,
With flowers intertwined in metal grille.
There's sweet abundance filling every space.
With untold joy we sing the Harvest hymns,
Our voices raised in dear, familiar tunes,
Appreciating all these wondrous things.

We thank you, God, with never-ending praise,
At Harvest-time and throughout all our days.

MY SOUTH SEA ISLAND

I love the view
    and look at sky
    all blue
    and streaked with apricot
    and jade
    reflected in
    the rippling sea.
I see the fringed palms
    waving on
    golden sand .....
    and feel a sense
    of wonder,
    for I
    have painted it.
I with my latent talent
    captured
    the exotic scene .....
    and feel God-kissed.

TO BETTY - THE GIFT OF A SON

Betty Waterfield opened the lounge window and shook out the bright, yellow duster. With great care she dusted the piano. Since Joe had gone it had never been played, but - even though she had left the old home two years and more ago - she had brought it with her, to Coppice Avenue.

It was pleasant to remember Joe sitting there, rattling out one bright tune after another. He could play anything - from jazz to Chopin. And nobody could equal his 'Amazing Grace'. He had a gift. For Joe had never had a piano lesson in his life.

And his life hadn't been long enough. Betty felt she would never understand why he had been taken with a heart attack at the age of fifty-two. It was something she often wondered about. But he had been perfectly fit right up to his death. No disease. No pain. No maddening loss of memory. With the passing years her deep sorrow had lessened. Though sometimes she missed him unbearably.

She picked up the photograph that always stood on the top of the piano, duster at the ready ..... but she made no move to use it. She just held the photograph, looking with love at the face laughing back at her. His fair hair fell in an unruly wave underneath his sailor's hat. His chin had a deep cleft in the middle, like that actor whose name she could never remember. A son any mother could be proud of. And Betty was proud.

For long minutes she held the photograph in her hands, and looked and looked. For once there was no answering smile on her face. She hadn't realised she was crying until a tear splashed on to the shining glass. Absently she wiped it off with her duster. Surely, surely, after all this time, they were not going to find her out?

Another tear squeezed through.

"*Oh Clive!*" she whispered. "*I couldn't live without you now. I couldn't. I just couldn't!*"

What was it Mrs Jenkins had said yesterday afternoon ..... ?

"*I can't understand your Clive being away, at sea, all these years. Especially without any home leave.*"

This was during the little whist drive, held in this very room.

And, last week, at Mrs Gray's, Mrs Bates had said: "*If I were you I'd write to the Admiralty. They've no right to keep a young man so long, especially as you're a widow.*"

Had it been her imagination, or had Mrs Bates exchanged a knowing look with Mrs Jenkins?

How she longed for the comfort of Joe's arms around her. But then, if Joe had still be alive, she wouldn't have needed Clive .....

It was just six weeks after Joe's heart attack, and she'd felt she just had to get out of the house. She had gone to the bus station and taken the first bus out, not caring where it was going. It had been to a picturesque town some thirty miles away. She had just meandered through the streets, idly looking in shop windows.

And that was when she saw the photograph.

It was as though there were no other photograph in the photographer's window. The laughing sailor was looking straight at her. She could feel his magnetism. She looked and looked.

How proud his mother must be to call him 'Son'.

Son!

Son! Why not?

Wherever she went women talked about their sons and daughters: daughters teaching nursery school, going to college, having babies. Sons in travel firms, playing in orchestras, journalists on local newspapers .....

And she ..... What had she to talk about? How clever Joe had been with his carving? The jewel box he'd made, with a water-lily on the lid? The time he'd played the piano in a restaurant? She'd tried it. Nobody had been interested. Nobody cared. All that was in the past. Their children were doing things now.

She was inside the shop before she realised she had moved.

"The photograph of the sailor? Is it for sale?"

Yes, it was one that had been taken, but never claimed.

Minutes later she walked out of the rather dim interior into bright sunlight, the precious parcel clutched tightly in her arms.

And all the way home she hugged it to herself, along with her secret.

Finding a name for him had been easy. Joe's middle name had been Clive. It recalled far-off school days and Clive of India. Had she had a son of her own, that's what they'd have named him.

It was hard to leave the house where she and Joe had been so happy, but she was starting a new life now, and it had to be in another town, where she wasn't known.

And the piano was the place for Clive's photograph.

Gradually Clive began to figure in Betty's conversation. She tried it out in a bus queue one morning. The woman in front of her was saying that her Ronald lived in America, where they didn't know what queues were.

Betty said: "*My Clive's been in America, but he's in Iceland now - the Navy, you know. When he's finished his time he's coming back to England, he says. No more foreign travel for him.*"

How easy it was!

The surprising thing was that, before long, she had acquired a nice little circle of friends. They'd meet in town for coffee, and they had intimate little whist drives in each other's houses. Between hands they talked about their families: Janet's new boy friend; Nick's rise to manager ..... and so on.

The first time they came to Betty's house everyone admired the photograph of Clive.

"*He looks a lively sort,*" someone commented, and Betty, with the merest catch in her voice, replied: "*Yes, he's a good son, is Clive. Always ready for a laugh. Full of mischief. Enjoys being in the Navy.*"

Strange how, with talking about him, and being so much in her thoughts, Clive had become as real to her as Mrs Bate's Richard, or Mrs Gray's Nick .....

_____

Betty held the photograph closer. Her hands trembled.

Clive belonged to her as surely as if she and Joe had brought him up from birth. She knew every detail of his character: his love for animals, his way of joking in times of stress or danger; the very inflexions of his voice .....

What was going to happen? She couldn't keep on making excuses, giving reasons why Clive hadn't been home in the last three years. Sooner or later she'd have to admit to the fact that Clive wasn't her son. That she'd never had a son. How could she possibly do it? How could she face the sneers, the ridicule? How could she expect them to understand?

"*I shall have to leave again,*" she whispered. "*I shall have to leave this darling house ..... this town ..... my friends .....*"

She jumped as a voice shouted: "*Hi, Ginger! Candy Floss! Where are you all? Aren't you going to see what the sea's washed up?*"

Wonderingly, Betty replaced the photograph, aware that she must have left the front door undone after taking the milk in. Someone had made a mistake. That was obvious.

She went into the hall ..... and stared, disbelieving.

"Oh, I'm sorry, Ma'm. Didn't know my friends the Milligans had left. Sorry to ....." The voice tailed off.

For the first time in her life, Betty knew she was going to faint.

She came round to find Clive bending over her, his face full of concern.

"Feeling better? Do you think we could get you on the settee? It can't be very comfortable on the carpet - though it's kinda pretty."

As though in a dream, Betty looked at the sailor, then at the photograph on the piano.

"Will someone tell me what this is all about?" he laughed. *"I'm all at sea! No. That's where I've come from ..... Maybe Ginger Milligan left my photo behind? But ..... they never had my photo ....."* He broke off, looking more bewildered than ever.

"What's your name?" asked Betty, feeling stronger every second.

"Clifford Mellors."

"Clifford!" She exclaimed in amazement. *"Clifford! Not so very different from Clive!"*

"You look as though you're recovering," Clifford said. *"And I owe you an explanation. My dear Mum and Dad were killed in a car crash over two years ago. It just about broke my heart, for we were very close. So I decided to opt for another period of service. I've been all over the world - which is why I lost touch with my friends, the Milligans. Now I've finished with the Navy I thought I might be able to stay with my pals overnight while I look for digs."* He paused. *"Now, will you tell me why you have my photo on your piano, and why my name's Clive."*

And, when she had finished telling him the whole story, her heart was already singing, for hadn't he told her that he'd lost his own Mum and Dad and was alone in the world?

The tears were in his eyes, too, by the time she finished. Silently they hugged.

Betty finally held him away from her and looked into his eyes. *"And you won't mind if I call you Clive?"*

"Mind?" he cried, hugging her all over again. *"Mind! Why, I'll love it - Mum."*

MY WORLD IS WONDERFUL!

I watch the flight
of a bird
like a poem
on the wind.

A tree is a symphony
in green
blazoning to
unimagined beauty
in the autumn.

Queen Anne's lace
gifts the wayside ditch,
florets enchant in
almost mathematical
perfection.

Bees, big and bumbly,
heavy with honey,
make music
among the marigolds.

Cotton clouds
skate across
ice-blue sky,
fantasy shapes,
ever-changing.

A caterpillar
on a nearby leaf
unknowingly
awaits
transformation.

My world is wonderful,
and I am
ever grateful.

THE BEGINNING - AND END - OF A FRIENDSHIP

They looked at me askance.
"John? That rude, hard man? Him?"
And widened eyes held shock at news
Of sudden death, but even greater shock
To know that he was my beloved friend,
And that I mourned him, heart a-drape
With crepe of deepest black.

He wasn't rude, or hard. I knew.
I'd seen those heavy shoulders shake with sobs
And watched the tears flow: seen loneliness
Look starkly from those haunted eyes.

I'd known his years were numbered, knew that
He knew, too, and hardly dared to
Look ahead to pain - a constant enemy -
Grown into giant, with tearing hands
And trampling feet,
Pitiless, all-powerful.

He wore a shell, did John, his 'carapace',
His shield from further hurt, deliberately,
Like costume of a clown,
And people shied away and never knew
The man who hid within.

God, in His Grace, showed me behind and underneath
That shell, and friendship sprang,
A veritable spring of life, between the two of us.
And love - the finest love of all,
That asks for nothing in return - flowed healingly,
And I discovered a man with heart so big,
Encompassing, kind, and blessed with understanding:
A poet, full of sensitivity, whose gift for words
Grew as our friendship grew.

And so, for just eleven months,
That spring welled forth in plenitude, and I knew then
That this was something fine, and beautiful, and good,
A richness given with open hands, a richness shared.

And then the letter came: *'Killed in a crash.*
His car swerved right across the road .....'

I'll always mourn for John, and yet I'll know
A debtedness that I prised off that ugly shell
And found, inside, a soul akin to mine.

This poem was the winner of the Tom Tyler Poetry Competition in 1989, but has not previously been published.

CHRISTMAS DAY

C   hrist Jesus, born in Bethlehem,

H   eralding new life for us,

R   eigning as King

I   n perpetuity,

S   erving His Father,

T   eaching His disciples, performing

M   iracles

A   nd dying on the cross for our

S   ins.

D   on't fail to celebrate His birth

A   nd worship Him in

Y   our hearts today and forever.

COMPENSATIONS

For many years I have been acutely aware of COMPENSATIONS. I believe there is a God-given law of compensations.

Way back an elderly relative had to go into hospital. She had become incontinent and very mixed up in her mind. It became impossible for her to be looked after at home.

Mrs X had not been an easy woman to love. The greater part of her life had been spent in moaning and groaning. Her excellent Home Help was called *'The Woman',* and blamed for everything, from scratches on the furniture to making coffee one morning ..... *"You know what she did that for? To give a hint that she wanted one."* I don't think she succeeded. The Vicar called. *"Just at tea-time. You can guess why."* He wasn't lucky, either.

So my husband and I daren't think of the many things she'd find to moan and complain about in hospital. We dreaded visiting her.

And what a surprise we had!

We were greeted excitedly with: *"The nurse took us all out for tea yesterday. We had cucumber sandwiches and cake. Such a nice cafe."*

Rather bewildered, because we knew she wasn't capable of getting out of bed by herself, let alone going out for tea, I asked which cafe it was.

"Marsden's," was her prompt reply.

And then we knew. Marsden's cafe had vanished years before. She had imagined the whole outing.

Every time we visited we were regaled with her adventures. Once Mrs X said, in a conspiratorial whisper: *"You'll never guess where we went to last night!"*

We couldn't.

"To a pub!"

I'm absolutely certain that Mrs X had never been inside a pub in her life. My husband played along. *"What did you have to drink? A sherry?"*

Mrs X pulled herself up to her full height - in bed. (She was a tiny woman) and, bursting with indignation, retorted: *"A sherry! I should think I did not have a sherry!"* But she had had a whale of a time, and knew that she, her fellow patients and the nurse, had been extremely naughty.

Our once-dreaded visits were looked forward to.

And an incredible thing happened. I found myself loving her. The impossible had happened.

God gives us these compensations. They crop up everywhere.

Following a phone call, Angela came to see me. She was seventeen and indescribably beautiful. She had blue eyes with curling lashes, golden hair, wavy and abundant. Her beauty shone from within. She was like a princess in a fairy story.

And she was crippled with arthritis. Her delicate hands had undergone operations. She had a finger-straightening gadget on each hand. Her feet were in irons.

And she was an incredibly gifted artist. Her drawings of horses were alive with movement. Yet, even on her good days, she could work no longer than 10 minutes at a time.

COMPENSATIONS.

A dear friend had suffered ill health for many years, yet was always cheerful.

One day I had such an excited letter. Something *'impossible'* had happened. Some friends had asked her to join them on a luxury cruise! - said the sea air would do her good. I could sense her utter amazement as she added: *"And all they want in exchange is my company! My company, Dolly!"*

COMPENSATIONS

Just as we would not appreciate beauty if there were no ugliness, or the majesty of a mountain if there were no valleys, I believe that we cannot know the heights of happiness unless we also know the meaning of suffering. By deep suffering we become capable of the most lark-soaring, God's-in-His-Heaven-and-all's-right-with-the-world joy and heavenly bliss.

Life is full of COMPENSATIONS.

I AM IMMORTAL

It never has made sense to me
    To think that on the day I die
I stop my living, cease to be,
    A light gone out, a heedless cry.

It's unacceptable that I -
    So full of life, so richly blessed,
So vital, so alive - should die
    And disappear to final rest.

The evidence around me make
    Sheer nonsense of this calumny,
When, annually, bright blossom breaks
    Like fragrant wave on hedge and tree.

Dark earth erupts with vivid flowers,
    Probed for nectar by honey-bee,
And grass is greener after showers,
    And butterfly emerges, free.

Abundant life is all around.
    But man was in God's image made.
I don't accept that we're earth-bound,
    Of less importance, lower grade.

I have a soul, an inner light.
    Nothing can ever put it out.
Life carries on within His sight.
    There never could be any doubt.

I opened my door
smiling a merry welcome
and Jesus stood there.

DEATH OF AN ASH TREE

The high-powered blade moved with unerring speed
Cutting off life with swift economy.
One moment my beloved tree raised shaggy branches to the sky,
The next it lay across the road, a dam
Blocking the way and making traffic halt.
Now busy hands and whining, sharp-toothed saw
Worked with rapid rhythm - cut and roll and cut and roll again -
Until the road was clear and cars were on the move.

A century and more that tree had stood
Gifting the road - once quiet country lane -
With bounteous grace and comeliness and pride,
Dwarfing almond tree and silver birch,
Bird-rich, alive with song:
Majestic, generous in summer leaf: decked in black lace
Or shimmering silver on winter days.

And now it stood no more that four feet high,
A body lopped of limbs, deprived of life.
No more would sap, a tingling force, surge through those
Outstretched arms. No more would Spring break forth
In palest green, nor Autumn splash her reds and gold.

Tears stung my eyes and bile rose in my throat.
I felt a desolation and a loss. Remorse took hold of me,
Relentless, hard.
I had done murder. I had killed this tree.
..... One windy night last year an eight-foot branch
came hurtling down and nearly took a life .....

The foreman, wood in hand, called me across
And bade me look at what the saw laid bare .....
And there they were, the tunnels, smooth and round, lacing
Throughout the length and breadth of tree, in parallels
And merging, gouged out tracks.

And then I saw the creeping crawling thing emerge
From sculpted cave into the light:
A black obscenity, a hideous filth
Whose appetite had wrecked my lovely ash.

The mists dispersed. No murder had I done.
The cut, so swift, so clean, had given dignity
And honey-sweet release from slow decay.
It died, as it had always lived -
A tree.

BE A BRIDGE-BUILDER

The notice-board outside the Methodist Church read:

'SOME LONELY PEOPLE BUILD WALLS INSTEAD OF BRIDGES.'

It's true! I thought. I know people who wait for others to visit them, never dreaming of doing the visiting themselves. They seem to make themselves difficult to reach, rather like the princess in distress in stories of medieval times, who wept crocodile tears behind the bars of a window high up in a castle tower. Anyone bent on rescue had to swim deep moats, climb castle walls and spiralling stone steps, then break down an iron-studded oak door.

Are you as inaccessible? Are you a wall-builder? Yes? Then put a stick of dynamite under those walls and demolish them right now!

Realise that self-help is your passport for getting out of that barred prison, the prison you made with your own hands and mind.

Decide: NO MORE WALLS. Be a BRIDGE BUILDER.

MAKE UP YOUR MIND TO LIVE

Make up your mind where you belong, and vow
to live your life more fully, banish fears,
Forget the yesterdays and live for now.
Forget those terrors of the past, the tears,
The unkind word, the vicious act, the wrongs,
For they are gone for good, will not return.
Lift up your heart and sing sweet, joyous songs,
Stoke up the fire of life and let it burn
With crimson glow and rich, soul-warming heat.
Create an atmosphere of love and light,
Ghosts gone for good, and people new to meet.
Go on, my friend, you know it's worth the fight.
 Live every second. Life is great, you'll find.
 It's up to you. Go on, make up your mind!

THE GIFT OF FLOWERS

The sight of snowdrops pushing through the soil,
Their milk-white bells so dainty and so pure,
Sweet messengers announcing: "Here is Spring!"
Are such delights, and there to reassure
That winter is, at last, on the way out
And Nature's re-awakening has begun.
Soon daffodils will gift the earth with gold
And tulips lift their petals to the sun.
The lilac trees flaunt blossom, mauve and white.
Laburnums trail their yellow fingers down
To point at polyanths in colours bright
And pansy in her richest velvet gown.
Come longer days, and marigolds appear,
And lavender and stocks perfume the air.
Clematis, starry-eyed, climb garden wall,
Then roses, richly red or creamy-fair.

And so, sunflower, carnation, peony,
Lupin and larkspur, Canterbury bell,
In sweet profusion grow in the dark earth
Gifting our sense of vision and of smell.

The wonder of it all my soul uplifts.
I bow my head and thank God for His gifts.

The carol-singers
sang like a heavenly choir -
and blessed my Christmas.

HUG!

Someone out there
needs
a hug.

Someone has shoulders
bowed
with sorrow,
is desperate
for
love and understanding.

Let God show you
the way.

Obey your
intuition
and when you find
the suffering one
reach out your arms,
open your heart ...

And HUG!

"Where's this mighty God?"
the pagan asked in triumph.
I held out a rose.

22

CURIOSITY

"Ask, and it shall be given you; seek, and ye shall find; knock, and it shall be opened unto you."   Luke 11:9.

Throughout our meal in a cafe, my family and I found our gaze wandering to a wooden plaque hanging on the wall. All it bore were the carved letters - 'YCHCYTFTB.' I had to know. "Please," I asked a passing waitress, "what do those letters stand for?"

Smiling mischievously she replied: "Your Curiosity Has Cost You Threepence For The Blind."

With delighted laughter, we paid up - though more than the stipulated threepence.

And I've never forgotten that plaque.

Curiosity is a wonderful thing. If you stop being curious, I reckon you've lost the joy of living. Life is so astonishing. To be wide-eyed isn't enough. By seeking knowledge we enlarge ourselves, and often benefit others.

Take Jenner, for instance, he became curious about cowpox. As a result smallpox, that once dreaded disease, has been practically wiped out.

Newton was curious seeing an apple falling to the ground ..... and discovered the law of gravity.

Watt looked at a boiling kettle, and wondered why the steam lifted the lid ..... and discovered the power of steam.

Researchers are at it all the time. The wondering about what happens if .....? Results in new ways of curing serious diseases.

Let's preserve the curiosity we had as children right through into adult life. Let's continue to ask, to seek, and to knock.

GOD'S LIGHT

If you switch on the light
  And no glimmer appears,
It's dark, for it's night,
  And you tremble with fear.

Find a torch, flick the switch .....
  Again, there's no light.
It's darker than pitch;
  You're in such a plight.

There's a candle somewhere,
  Maybe in the front room.
That's good! Put it there,
  It will lessen the gloom.

A blown bulb is useless,
  And batteries run down.
A candle is worthless
  If no matches are found.

We're lit from within
  With the love of our Lord.
It shines everlasting:
  He gave us His Word.

So, don't get disheartened
  When trouble draws near,
Know that God is your Friend
  And His Light's always here.

---

*Grey clouds swept the sky
blotting out the noon-day sun
momentarily.*

TUNE IN TO INSPIRATION

"And he turned unto his disciples, and said privately, Blessed are the eyes which see the things that ye see; For I tell you, that many prophets and kings have desired to see those things which ye see, and have not seen them: and to hear those things which ye hear, and have not heard them."

Luke 10:23-24.

I had been to the BBC in London to record a radio talk and was returning home by train. It rained the entire journey.

Suddenly I noticed a small phenomenon. It was raining so hard, and the train was travelling at such a speed, that the raindrops were travelling horizontally across the carriage window. And these raindrops wiggled their way from left to right exactly like shoals of little tadpoles! I was entranced. Wiggle wiggle, wiggle wiggle, they went. Fat little heads and long, wiggly tails. Just like the ones I used to catch and bring home in a jam jar when I was a child.

Desperately I wanted to say to somebody: "Look at those little tadpoles!" And, no doubt, be thought mad!

But I'm a writer. I have to communicate.

Hurriedly I delved into my handbag, found a couple of envelopes, slit them open ..... and began writing.

Unbeknown to me I had become a boy of eight, travelling on a train between London and Nottingham. His parents had been killed in a car crash and he was going to live with his godmother. A most unusual story. I lived it. And it all began with those wiggly little tadpoles.

I wrote madly and had almost finished it when the train arrived in Nottingham.

I titled the completed story 'DESTINATION NOTTINGHAM', and broadcast it on BBC Radio Nottingham.

Once again - for it happens frequently - I had been inspired.

We can all use this God-given inspiration. It is limitless. All we need are those seeing eyes and hearing ears. We tune in ..... and God does the rest.

SHINE!

Not everyone can be a star,
But each one has a light.
Just think about the glow-worm
That lights the hedge at night.

Your shining light might be your smile,
And every bit as bright,
Especially to somebody
Who needs that kind of light.

Your eyes are windows of the soul
And God-light shines out clear,
So look with love on those you meet
And see how much you cheer.

Remember how, as little child,
You sang that lovely hymn -
'Jesus bids us shine' - and so
Shine beacon-bright for Him.

HIS LOVE IS WONDERFUL

God must love us, to give us so much:
Sweet flowers to smell, a kitten to touch:
Mountains and sunset, bird-song and trees,
The smiles of a baby, honey from bees.
We laugh and we love: we dance and we sing.
We're dazzled with blossom every Spring.
We're blessed with talents; artistic skills,
Landscapes to paint, make silk daffodils.
There's music to make, or pots from clay,
Swimming or walking, and games to play.
He loves us, it's true, in so many ways,
Let's thank our dear Lord and give Him due praise.

A PRAYER FOR TODAY

Thank you, God,
for today:
a smooth sheet of life
for us to write on.
May that writing be inspired.
Thank you for
the wholeness
of this day,
from blossoming dawn
to fragrant dusk
and through the night hours.
Thank you for each
second of each minute
of every hour.
May we use them
all wisely
and to your good.

Thank you, God,
for this gift of
today.
May we take it
and <u>live</u> it.

          Amen.

---

*The parachutist
jumped from the plane and landed
in His loving arms.*

27

ENGLAND, MY ENGLAND

Sylvan lanes, sunlight-filtered,
  Brown earth dappled through the leaves,
Honey bees and climbing roses,
  Scarlet poppies, golden sheaves.

Lusty oaks and acorns tiny,
  Blackbirds singing in blue sky,
Buttercups and ragged robin,
  Barley growing, wheat and rye.

Rock-strewn shores and foaming breakers,
  Sculpted mountains, dreamy dales,
Heather glowing in the sunset,
  Poplars lashing in the gales.

Such the beauty of this England,
  Silver-threaded mile on mile.
Jade and ruby, gold and sapphire,
  Jewel-crowned - my precious isle.

*Just when the storm breaks
and thunder cracks likes cannon
God sends His rainbow.*

A TWO-WAY GIVING

It was the Minister's morning to visit Mrs Smith, who, because of severe arthritis, found it very difficult getting about. She had been a teacher, and the Minister knew how frustrated she must be feeling.

He let himself in and was greeted, as always, cheerily and with tea and biscuits.

"I wonder if you could help me out," he began. "I've met a couple of students attending University, and I think they would enjoy visiting you and, maybe, you'd help them with their English? One's Japanese, the other from Malaya. Really nice young men, very well mannered. As you can imagine, they get pretty lonely, being so far from home and their families."

Mrs Smith's eyes shone. "There's nothing I'd like better," she told her Minister. "Give them my phone number and tell them to get in touch, and we'll fix a first date."

The Minister was delighted. "I knew you'd help out," he said. "Thank you so much."

He then drove to a house a couple of streets away, used by students from abroad, and knocked on the door. "Hello Kouchi, Masami, I've just been to see one of my elderly members whose arthritis keeps her pretty well housebound. She's an intelligent lady, ex-school-teacher. But lonely. Would you please visit her occasionally? She'd really appreciate it. This is her phone number."

That Minister knew a thing or two about human nature. We all like to be helpful, but don't always know how to go about it. Sometimes we need showing the way.

And, in no time at all, Mrs Smith had become an adopted Granny to two young foreign students.

TIME

If I had the time, a writer I'd be:
Detective novels - I like mystery.
I'd begin with short stories, or poetry .....
      If only I had the time.

If I had the time, a painter I'd be:
Landscapes and sunsets, and boats by the sea,
Roses and castles, hoar-frost on a tree .....
      If only I had the time.

If I had the time, a pianist I'd be.
I'd play Chopin, jazz, a sweet melody.
I might even get to play on T.V! .....
      If only I had the time.

Writers, painters, and pianists, my dear,
Like you, have fifty-two weeks in a year,
And twenty-four hours in each day. It's clear .....
      It's up to you to <u>make</u> time.

Lost and lonely I
walked into an empty church -
and there stood Jesus.

30

GOD'S ENDLESS GIFTS

The day was ending. Soon it would be dark.
In twilight hush I opened my back door .....
And saw the rose. My breath caught in my throat.
It seemed to glow from some deep inner core,
A shining coral pink amid the gloom.
And, as I stared, the sun slipped from the sky -
Yet, still, the rose glowed like some earthly star.
And ..... could it be I heard the garden sigh?

One night, whilst drawing curtains in my room,
I saw a cloud-form towering high and wide,
Magnificent, like ancient castle wall,
Where knights in shining armour used to ride.
I stood entranced, and hardly dared to move,
The feeling strong in me that God was near,
That He had richly gifted me again
With sights He knew that I would hold most dear.

These are but two of endless gifts received.
So many times I have to stand and stare
In awe and wonder at the things I see.
With gratitude I bow my head in prayer.

A tiny sparrow
fell from its nest one day
right into my heart.

MIRACLE AT CHRISTMAS
A true story

Betty's five-year-old daughter was to appear in her first Nativity Play. Each year, Miss Smedley, the Headmistress of the Infants School, wrote a musical play, guaranteed to hold the interest of both children and parents. Her plays were different! One year she even incorporated Robin Hood and his Merry Men - for this was a school in Nottingham.

Betty wondered whether her father would enjoy it. Whether, in fact, he'd get anything out of it at all, for he had suffered three strokes in two years, had lost the power of speech and was partially paralysed. All his outings were in a wheel chair. But Betty thought it worth a try.

"Of course we can accommodate your father," said Miss Smedley.

Came the day. As Betty wheeled her father across the playground, Miss Smedley came outside, in the biting cold, and manoeuvred the chair into an ideal position, right beside the beautifully decorated Christmas tree.

The play began. The story of the birth of our Lord Jesus unfolded. Betty kept looking at her father. He seemed to be enjoying it. In fact he looked as though he didn't want to miss a single word or action: one note of their singing.

"And do you know", Betty told me, the next time I saw her, "he's never stopped talking about it since!"

I needed a friend.
I felt so lonely and lost.
Meow! My needs were met.

WARM-HEARTED, not MARBLE COLD

Passing a church, one morning, I read, on the 'Wayside Pulpit' - 'Carve your name on hearts, not marble', and I have never forgotten it.

Marble is cold, hard, inanimate. I knew then, as I know now, that I want no sculpted headstone. I want to occupy places in people's hearts.

God is love. We reflect that love. Sometimes we are so filled with love that 'our cup runneth over'. And the wonderful thing is that, no matter how much love we give, we are never love-empty. Always there is more.

So, in those far-off years, when our names come up in conversation, let there be warm smiles, a lifting of hearts, and bright faces.

Spread love and caring, kindness and happiness today, and words on tombstones will be superfluous. We'll live on forever in the hearts of those who knew us.

---

*If you see somebody without a smile on their face,
why not give them one of yours?*

Keep your face to the sunshine and you cannot see the shadows.

THE CHOICE IS YOURS

Are You A King or A Slave?

"Life is the mirror of king and slave. If we see ourselves as kings, we rule. If we see ourselves as slaves, we are continually in bondage. LIFE REFLECTS BACK TO US WHAT WE BELIEVE ABOUT OURSELVES."

I read these words in a recent issue of ABUNDANT LIVING, and the Truth jelled. I could name numerous people who, this very moment, are seeing slaves in their mirrors and who, consequently, are living what I call non-lives.

And, suddenly, in my mind, I was at a wedding. The hosts were most concerned to realize that they had no wine. Jesus was one of the guests. He called for water ..... and he turned that water into wine.

In turn, I was present - in that visualizing mind of mine - when Jesus gave sight to a blind man: healed a leper: made whole a man's withered arm: fed five thousand people with five loaves and two fishes ..... I have always loved reading about the miracles Jesus performed.

Recently, planning a one day Seminar titled "PROGRAMME YOURSELF FOR ABUNDANCE." I found myself asking: Why did Jesus give sight to the blind man? Why did he heal the leper? Why did he return to wholeness that man's withered arm? Why did he feed those five thousand? Why did he turn water into wine at that wedding feast? Why, in fact, did he perform all his miracles?

Didn't he say (John 10:10) *I am come that they might have life and they might have it more abundantly?*

And it came to me, like a lightning flash: Jesus wanted ABUNDANCE for these people. He knew they could not be abundant if they were blind, or diseased, or hungry. And he wanted them to be whole and healthy and abundant, living life to the full.

It has always intrigued me that Jesus turned water into wine at that wedding in Cana of Galilee. He could so easily have said: "What's wrong with water? Water is good for you. Animals drink water, and look how strong they are. Forget the wine. What are you complaining about?"

But he didn't.

Jesus wants only the best for us. He wants us to be strong and in good health, enjoying a full life. An abundant life.

That message comes across to me loud and clear.

If we have abundance we are much better equipped to bring abundance to others. If we are happy, we can bring happiness to others. If we have energy, we can use that energy for others. If we have money, we can spend it on those less fortunate. If it were not for successful people, who do you think would finance and support many other worth-while causes and charities? So don't think it wrong to have money.

One morning, listening to my radio, I heard a group of elderly citizens being interviewed. A man in his late seventies was asked: "To what do you attribute your good health and that lively sparkle in your eyes?"

"Well," said the man. "Every morning when I wake up, I have two choices: to be happy, or sad. Naturally I choose to be happy."

He'll be loved and wanted, by his children and grandchildren. He'll have won warm places in their hearts. For what he puts into life, he'll receive back from it ..... a hundredfold. For this is a law.

We all know the old saying: "God helps those who help themselves." Aren't we all much more willing to help somebody if they are already making an effort themselves?

What do you see when you look in the mirror? A king? ..... Or a slave?

"Prove that there's a God!"
he cried. And up in the sky
a bright rainbow arched.

LIFE - A CHALLENGE

Why did the man with no roof to his mouth become a preacher?

Why did the blind man become a reporter?

Why did the woman with no arms become a telephone operator?

Why did the man with no elbows become a violinist?

Why did the deaf girl become a percussionist?

And why did all those men and women born without arms and hands, or with useless, paralysed hands, become artists, with a brush gripped between their teeth or toes?

Wouldn't a man with a speech impediment choose any job rather than one in which he had to speak in public?

Wouldn't a blind person go in for basket-making rather than going out into the world reporting on events he couldn't see?

Wouldn't the young woman born without arms feel that, of all jobs, being a telephonist on a firm's telephone exchange was quite beyond her? But no, she operated the switches with her toes.

Wouldn't the Viennese man know that he'd need elbows to play a violin? He was a brilliant player.

And all those people born without arms and hands, or with paralysed limbs feel that painting, of all things, was quite beyond them?

What wonderful courage these people have! So often, it seems, physically handicapped people do far more than we, who have all our faculties. Is life a greater challenge for them? Are they determined to succeed against all odds?

And I remember a well-known saying: 'God helps those who help themselves'.

How God must love these people!